The Language of Cancer

The Language of Cancer

Poems by

Caroline Johnson

© 2025 Caroline Johnson. All rights reserved.
This material may not be reproduced in any form, published,
reprinted, recorded, performed, broadcast,
rewritten, or redistributed without
the explicit permission of Caroline Johnson.
All such actions are strictly prohibited by law.

Cover design by Shay Culligan
Cover image by Alexa Frangos
Copyright: Alexa Frangos
Author photo by Linda Diaz

ISBN: 978-1-63980-742-0

Kelsay Books
502 South 1040 East, A-119
American Fork, Utah 84003
Kelsaybooks.com

for Bill

Praise for *The Language of Cancer*

Caroline Johnson weaves an array of topics through a common thread: an old boiler is swapped out for a new furnace, the close call of her husband on a ladder that didn't fall, an encounter with a bear in the backcountry that leaves hikers unscathed. While weighing out her personal what ifs, Johnson drives down the on ramp, merging boldly into chancy traffic with her foot on the gas pedal. Her poems apply a courageous language to her battle, with a unique sense of humor and wonder despite one of life's most serious experiences.

—Cynthia Gallaher, poet and author of *Frugal Poets' Guide to Life*

With powerful imagery and reflections, Caroline Johnson's words trace the pain, fear, yearning, and even beauty that comes with a cancer diagnosis. *The Language of Cancer* provides an invitation to reflection and encouragement to continue moving forward towards hope, gratitude, and joy in the face of cancer. I am touched by the power of Caroline's words and trust that readers will find solace and inspiration in these poems.

—Ellen Nieman, MSW, LCSW, Oncology Social Worker / Associate Director of Programs, Wellness House. Hinsdale, Illinois

Acknowledgments

I am grateful to the editors from these journals and anthologies who first selected the following poems for publication in print or online, some in different versions.

ADVERSITY Anthology: "The Power of Pink," "Driving Through the Dark," "The Guillotine"
BezzyBC (Healthline.com): "Cancer," "Thoughts Before My Mastectomy," "The Last Toy"
Blanket Sea Magazine: "The Second Arrow"
Distilled Lives: "March," "Rain"
DuPage Valley Review: "The Guillotine"
East on Central: "Corn Maze"
Encore: Prize Poems: "Boiler," "Cancer," "Ladder"
The Fairy Tale Magazine: "Mermaid in the Garden"
FRIENDS & FRIENDSHIP Anthology: "She Says Blue Looks Good on Me"
The Hands We Hold: "Resistance"
I Come From the World: "Thoughts Before My Mastectomy," "Refuge"
Light4ph.org: "The Language of Cancer"
Naugatuck River Review: "Chasing Bees"
Oddball Magazine: "Veteran's Day"
Pink Panther: "Rowing"
Pure Slush: "Corn Maze"
Recovering the Self: "Modlitwa"
Seers & Sibyls Anthology: "The Healer"
Still Point Arts Quarterly: "Tai Chi"
Tuck Magazine: "To the 800,000 DACA Children, from One Cancer Survivor"
Turtle Island Quarterly: "April in Garden of the Gods"
Verse-Virtual: "Moon Walk," "Amazons," "The Last Toy," "Last of the Seers," "At the Plaza del Carmen in Madrid."

Poets & Patrons Chicagoland Poetry Contest:
"Modlitwa" (2022), "At the Plaza del Carmen in Madrid" (2021), "Dance of the Adders" (2020, 1st Place, Nature Category), "Prayer" (2018, 2nd Place, Religious), "At the Surgeon's Office" (2018, 2nd Place, Free Verse).

National Federation of State Poetry Societies (NFSPS) Contest:
"Boiler" (2017, 2nd Place, NFSPS Board Award), "Ladder" (2018, 3rd Place, Freeda Murphy Memorial Award), "Cancer" (2019, 2nd Place, William Stafford Memorial Award).

I wish to thank the first readers of this manuscript, who helped shape it: Robin Smith Chapman, Wilda Morris, Cynthia Gallaher, Georgiann Foley, Vaunceil Kruse, and Darlene Norton. Special thanks to Vaunceil and Georgiann for their critical eye and countless hours discussing the manuscript. Thanks also to Pamala Dean, who has been my "writing buddy" for years on zoom.

Many thanks also to the Illinois State Poetry Society for their helpful critiques, especially the Darien critiquing group, and Chicagoland Poets & Patrons for their contests and workshops that kept me writing. I wrote many of these poems while I was undergoing treatment, so a huge thanks to my oncologists as well, especially Dr. Jay Dalal from UChicago Medicine AdventHealth.

In addition, thank you to Wellness House, a cancer non-profit that helped sustain me while I was writing these poems. I benefited from their many nutrition, cooking, exercise, and networking classes.

A big thank you to Karen Kelsay for believing in the manuscript and seeing it to fruition. And to my sisters, Brenda Ellis and Becky McLaughlan, for their love and support throughout my cancer journey. Finally, my partner in crime, Bill, for his tireless role in coaching me through difficult times, keeping me sane, and believing in me as a writer.

Contents

Preface	19
Mermaid in the Garden	25

I. Before

A Supreme Love	29
PINK: Part I	30

II. Fear

At the Surgeon's Office	33
Boiler	34
Moon Dance	35
The Last Toy	36
The Guillotine	37
Ladder	38
Inside	39
Bears	40
Driving Through the Dark	41
Rain	42
Life	43
PINK: Part II	44
After Reading Dorothy Parker	45

III. Treatment

Chasing Bees	49
Thoughts Before My Mastectomy	51
Radiation	53
Cancer, Part I	54

Resistance	55
Surfacing	57
Pink Slime	58
Echocardiogram	59
Cancer, Part II	61
Our Lover	62
Metamorphosis	63
The Second Arrow	65

IV. Recovery

Slumber	71
Descending	72
Sparrow	73
March	74
Amazons	75
Dance of the Adders	77
Spuds	78
She Says Blue Looks Good on Me	79
Tai Chi	80
Moon Walk	82

V. Spirit

The Healer	85
Last of the Seers	87
Samskaras	88
Wind Warrior	89
Blood Falls	90
My Wound	91
Circles	92

Modlitwa   93
Prayer   94
The Other Garden: A Haibun   95
Freedom   96

VI. Survival

Flight   99
The Language of Cancer   100
Refuge   103
How to Kill Cancer   104
Rowing   105
On Our 20th Wedding Anniversary   106
Corn Maze   108
Sonography of a Survivor   109
Not Alone   114
To the 800,000 DACA Children, from One Cancer Survivor   115
Veteran's Day   117
Soldier at College   119

VII. After

April in Garden of the Gods   123
At the Plaza del Carmen in Madrid   124
The Power of Pink   126

Notes   127

*For last year's words belong to last year's language,
and next year's words await another voice.*

—T.S. Eliot, *Four Quartets*

It is a river, this language.

—Carl Sandburg, "Languages"

Preface

On a recent trip to Eastern Europe with friends, I lit a candle in an orthodox church and prayed for good health. A priest blessed me, and I drank holy water from a plastic bottle the whole day.

The chapel was part of Belgrade's fortress, and was encased in light from candles, with a picture of a saint on the alter that I was to learn was Saint Petka, an 11th-century Serbian saint who was the protector of the sick, the poor, and women. She was believed to bring health, happiness, and miracles to those who prayed and believed in her. She was said to heal people.

As we learned about Serbian history, I couldn't help but compare the beleaguered country to a cancer patient. Belgrade fell to the Turks in 1521; the Austrians in the 18th and 20th centuries; the Nazis during WWII; the communists shortly thereafter. They participated in a bloody civil war in the 1990s, emerging from dictator Tito's vise-like grip after his death to establish their own identity.

Cancer also can feel like an invasion, a catastrophe to the country of your body. Such trauma provokes one to search for answers. For me, I turned to poetry. I wrote from when I was diagnosed with breast cancer on July 1, 2016, all the way through my surgery, chemo, and radiation. Then, I continued to write. As I became educated about cancer, as I started not to be afraid to talk about everything that had happened to me, I began to learn how to be my own advocate.

My parents both had lingering illnesses, Parkinson's and Alzheimer's, and I was the family caregiver. I served as their advocate to nurses, doctors, hospice professionals, social workers, etc. It was a tough role, a labor of love, but I can honestly say that I've found it much more challenging to be my own advocate. To learn how to navigate the different treatment options; to make decisions; to learn to trust your doctors; to spend countless evenings researching online.

These poems were a saving grace. They helped me in a way no person could. I had to take a break in the middle. I would write, continue treatment, then write more, then get more treatment. Afterwards, it was difficult to go back and revise, to "reenter" the dark abyss of cancer. I procrastinated, reluctant to read about cancer—MY cancer—even though these were moments of strength and courage. So much to fight against, so much angst, so much fear.

I began to write articles for an online community dedicated to breast cancer, BezzyBC, a platform of Healthline.com. My articles ranged from who do I tell about my cancer; clinical trials; how to get a second opinion; creativity and cancer; poetry and cancer; and finally, joy, gratitude, and how to face fear with courage.

Fear can lead to depression and anxiety. One way to combat fear, I have learned, is to stay busy. Whether it is doing mundane activities such as housework, playing with my cats, playing music, or going to work, all of these keep my mind from dwelling in a dark place. However, even better is finding your passion and focus. For me, my passion has always been my writing.

As a poet, I straddle two worlds: reality and fantasy. With my pen, a symbol, I dip into the word bank of my mind. I connect with spirit and the unconscious. As a cancer patient, I struggle to remain positive despite some dark reality. Not just my medicine helps me, but living each day, moment by moment, helps to accrue a sense of gratitude and delight with the present. I fight against a dark supernatural world, so that I can stay afloat like a mermaid in my own warm sea of deep subconsciousness.

The silver lining of cancer is gratitude and joy. I have learned to live each day, rather than constantly look into the future. Joy is the opposite of fear. It is living in the moment, feeling life through all your senses, finding meaning and purpose, finding flow.

Cancer can be a teacher, if you let yourself be a student. I have learned how to gather my gratitude, how to maximize love with the people around me, and with my writing. As the ancient philosopher Ovid said: "Chance is always powerful. Let your hook be always cast; in the pool where you least expect it, there will be fish." If you stay positive and work on your creativity, joy is sure to visit you. And, the more you do it, the better chance you have that joy will stay.

Traveling can also bring joy. To experience another culture is to experience another life—and so much history. We all could benefit from that, whether we have cancer or not. And who knows? Maybe you'll stumble upon some holy water too that has been blessed by a priest.

According to Japanese novelist Haruki Murakami, we all need a "quiet ability to focus," a "staying power that doesn't get discouraged, and a consciousness that is, up to a point, firm and systematic." My poetry has been an attempt to find that focus. I hope it helps you find it too, whether you have cancer, or have been touched by it in some way.

Remember this Native American saying when you are struggling:

The Elder: "Inside each of us are two wolves—a good wolf and a bad wolf. These wolves are always in battle—they are always at war within us throughout our lives."

The Youth: "Which wolf wins?"

The Elder: "The one you feed."

Caroline Johnson
April, 2025

Mermaid in the Garden

Do flowers mourn?
    —Linda Pastan

Outside your castle I get lost: purple coneflowers,
the pop of black-eyed Susans, cup plants that hold
rain, bee balm, blazing stars, milkweed, pink cosmos,
giant golden sunflowers. I am a mermaid growing
pollinators on my chest, with flowers instead
of breasts. I am no longer a nude pygmy.

I clutch my necklace, a small iron anchor.
My new legs stab like swords. I am overboard
on your music, my prince, drunk on longing
and brine, listening to your guitar riffs.
I have swallowed some of the sky and sun,
captured a jar of light, spread it onto the stars.

I hide in the nautilus of your heart, but Cancer's
hook cut the corner of my mouth and I have lost
all sense of time, tasting only blood and metastasis.

I stop to smell a wild rose, finger a Joe Pye weed,
wink at butterfly bushes. I don't remember anything
of Cancer's rape, but its fruit grows in my womb.

Will I return to the sea? I don't know. I spread my arms,
close my eyes, feel the presence of hummingbirds drinking
nectar, goldfinches as they feed on seeds. I miss saltwater,
the way seaweed tangled my hair, how I embraced
waves like Aphrodite, my tail glittering as I swam.

But how can I ever leave your garden? Can I even
question a love so blue it transcends time? I reach
inside, shove Cancer's fetus deep under rock, then dive
into the sea and swim towards the father of my tumor,
a pirate who trapped me deep below in darkness.

Your flowers will fade, my prince, like a sandcastle
washes away. But the perennials come back.
I, too, will reappear in foam and flora,
surfacing always to listen to your music.

I. Before

A Supreme Love

I am waiting to fly with you
into the cool blue of Chicago's
saxophonists, your beautiful bones,
shiny naked skin, my virgin white
breasts, staccato laughter.

I am waiting to dive with you
into Lake Michigan's navy splendor
populated with coho and pike, past
palisades that echo ancient Ojibwe,
bottom carp feasting on loneliness.

Let us go to an outdoor jazz fest
ten years before we first met,
wrestle on a stadium blanket,
listen as John Coltrane riffs
his way to a supreme love.

Come with me, past steel skyscrapers
into ancient aboriginal landscapes
away from whispers of sorrow
into the fused amalgam of time
until our song surfaces and appears.

PINK: Part I

It's the color of girly girl
the language of valentines
Victoria's Secret
bubbles and lace.

It protects you
in a warm embrace.

Pale pink baby shoes
crocheted sweaters
pastel roses
keep you chaste

but locked inside
a fragile cage.

Mother planted daffodils
and Amarillo tulips
wore yellow sweaters, hats,

her favorite color,
Marilyn Monroe's hair.
She gave me

unsupervised play time
where I could wear
any color I liked

except pink.

II. Fear

At the Surgeon's Office

She is a very intelligent woman who speaks slowly,
this doctor who clutches the black frames of her glasses
while leaning into her chair, the room silent as an autopsy
as she ushers forth the word *positive,* which means
neither that the weather is sunny nor that my life
had been pretty good so far. My husband, affectionate.
My cat, loyal. My friends, affirming. My work, gratifying.
Rather, it is a hint that my body has betrayed me—
not once, but twice—as two biopsies came back *positive.*
I can't help but wonder when the cells first went rogue.
Was it on my wedding day, my bust filling a strapless
ivory dress, my braided hair hidden behind a floor-length
Priscilla of Boston veil, my neck sporting my sister's
borrowed pearls? Or was it while hitchhiking through
Ireland and Scotland when my body became a foreign
country? Or during one of the many times I camped
with a canoe in the backcountry of upper Minnesota,
the threat of black bears as real as a tumor? Or perhaps
it was long ago while skiing out of bounds in Wyoming's
fresh powder that my cells first multiplied, forming
silent malignant moguls on my chest, that led to this day
in the doctor's office where I now feel my whole life derail.

Boiler

The boiler sits in our basement,
a dinosaur with asbestos still wrapped
around a pipe. We need a new boiler.
"It's as old as the house," my brother-in-law said.
That means it is probably more than 60 years old.
I don't know. I don't know anything about boilers,
except radiant heat is supposed to be better than
forced air. I do know I need to get rid of this
cancer that has taken over my left breast.
How I yearn for radiant air, for clean blood
that doesn't have to be drawn and tested
every month. I don't know. I need to get rid
of our boiler, but it still works. Perhaps if
I don't do anything and just let my body
do its thing, I will outlive our boiler.
I don't know. The boiler turns on and off
at its own tempo. It sends heat out in the
winter, but in the summer it sleeps.
It's always been reliable, and it has never
broken down. Perhaps in that way, I am not
like our boiler. Still, you get kind of attached
to it, like you get used to your body.
I wouldn't mind getting a new boiler.
In fact, I could even settle for a furnace,
if that's the way things turned out.

Moon Dance

When I brush my teeth each morning,
the sun blinds through clear glass
and I understand what the rays
are trying to say: *Slow down. Listen.*
Concentrate on seeing and breathing.

When the moon is at least half full,
illuminating the dark outline of the trees,
when our house is showered with moon,
sometimes I hear a coyote howl. But I
have never understood lunar language.

And now, more than half a century
of looking at moons, my throat aches
to spell out the letters on my breath—
*c-a-n-c-e-*r—to pilot them into a muddy
ravine and walk away. But I cannot.

Like the moon, my tumor is a foreign
country. I study its dead landscape,
attempt to move my mind to a safe
space, allow it to dance until darkness
disappears into the rich night light.

The Last Toy

The ribbon is orange, tied noose-like
a party ribbon that once prettied
our birthday presents.

And my cat can't get enough of it
as she tries again and again
sometimes missing it entirely
biting the air, her blind eyes wide
open, triumphant, when her teeth
capture the bow at last.

The vet assistant talked about shaving
part of her fur on one leg so a port
can be fitted more easily under her skin.

I wonder if her port will feel like mine.
My breast cancer, her lymphoma
is something we experience together.
She will not know how it feels
to die of cancer. I can spare her
that knowledge if the doctor
can cleanly inject the lethal dose
that will send her to Empyrean.*

But for now, my Persian is playing
as I recite poetry and shake this ribbon.
How have I pet thee? Let me count the ways.
I hold her close; she licks my finger as I say
one more Good Morrow to her waking soul,
'til it's time to let her go.

*Empyrean relates to the highest heaven and was believed to contain pure light or fire.

The Guillotine

A guillotine hovers over my head.
Wherever I go, it follows. Like my cancer,
it is omnipresent—sharpened, polished—
it can fall at any moment with the slightest
whim. If I run over a raccoon, it shivers.
If I stay motionless in my room, it rattles,
swinging side to side like a kite. I creep
on tiptoe, walk over a fire's hot coals,
lie down on a park bench with the hoboes,
and still it never leaves. Indeed, I can watch
the entire opera *Carmen* with my guillotine
beside me, feeling helpless, a victim, until
finally the guillotine leads me into its home,
a dark cave. The ceiling looks like a jewelry box.
It is cold; nobody lives there, and nothing grows
except things that grow in the dark, fungi,
things that shun the sun or are buried alive.

I search for secrets on the walls where natives
wrote cryptic messages long ago. As I melt
into the cave, the dark womb of the world,
my breasts become hollows, my hair, shiny
stalactites and dark loam. I offer myself
to the guillotine, welcome the lacerating
brutality to my body. Soon my teeth are
broken, my eyes bruised and black. I let
the guillotine spelunk my secret desires
until I find a weapon—laughter—to
destroy its immense shoulder, its absurd
razor. I laugh until my eyes are soaked,
then look up to see the guillotine has gone.

Ladder

—after James Wright

The sun is shining
and spills onto the leaf-covered
lawn this late afternoon. The near empty
trees, gaunt like used toothpicks, foreshadow
winter and death. Outside the window I see
a green ladder leaning on the house like a sentinel
guarding the sun. Earlier, my husband had climbed
it, shaky like the autumn leaves littering
our gully. He tried to empty the gutters,
but the ladder was not tall enough.
There is a trick to it. It is not rickety
and he did not fall, but still, like my cancer,
there was the fear.

A plane flies overhead, ferrying passengers
to the next life. I have wasted time
worrying about death and killing flies.

A dog barks from a nearby house.
At the end of the yard, a pipe pours
rainwater from our gutters into a muddy ravine.
I lean back onto the sofa, listen to the silence
and remind myself that he did not fall.

Inside

Jerry walks on the lawn
unravels brown rope,
attaches it to a pulley
hoists it up a tree.

Inside my body
a dark knot grows
gets thicker and more
bulbous, tines of density
replicating and replicating.

He pulls the rope higher,
towing the bird house
to the top branch.
It spins and spins
in tiny circles.

Soon, sparrows and cardinals
will be feeding on seeds.

My tumor feasts on estrogen
which could be lurking
in my blood. Like a hawk,
thoughts circle and circle
cawing loudly inside
as I wait for cancer
to make up its mind.

Bears

—along the Gunflint Trail, upper Minnesota

I

Walking down an empty dirt road
there is the fear of
black bears.

Each stone, puddle,
muddied pond reveals
shadows, secrets
of ourselves—

hidden, black,
appearing when we
least expect them—
our dark fears,
hungry carnivores
that devour
reason.

II

The first night here
a bear tried to get into our truck.
Jerry saw muddy paw prints in the morning.

Like cancer left imprints on my body
furiously replicating cells,
dirty windows to the soul—

the bear only touched the car
perhaps he rocked it back and forth.
Still, just knowing it came so close.

Driving Through the Dark

Driving through the dark I write poems
—Linda Pastan

I grip the steering wheel, attempt to merge
onto a busy Chicago expressway at night.
Heavy rain pounds my windshield.
A stalled truck blocks the ramp ahead,
its red light blinking. I break, panicked,

look to the left side mirror. Headlight
after headlight shoots past. Then a sudden
moment of darkness, a lickity quick
decision to step on the gas, veer left,
plunge the car into frightening speed.

Sometimes I dodge thoughts of cancer
by moving my mind across the fugitive
artery of memory's traffic, spin full
force through midnight's storm
of black terror—past night, past
dawn, past the reckless speed

of furious replicating cells,
maneuvering towards a growing
vocabulary of poetry that murmurs
a path towards luminescence.

Rain

Wet pellets ping my windshield as I drive on an expressway in the rain. A truck stalls, then an angry driver in a Corvette cuts me off, another whips along at dangerous speed. I need to wrap my arms around the space in front of me, glide on the highway, my tires now ice skates, the freezing rain sprinkling my windows like raw rice at a wedding. Just one wrong move, one turn into a concrete tunnel, one bare-faced bold acceleration, and I can almost hear the crunch of metal fabricated turbo engines, can feel the hot balloons as they unburden a soft pillow to my frightened face, not the lesson in loss I want to learn, but fear of an accident almost as strong as the terror of cancer, melting into the conclusion that we all will die, so simple to realize I will join the parade's end, the giant Goofy, Donald Duck, Micky Mouse, Barney, soon to be cadavers in the ground, my ashes thinly scattered across some vibrant poppy garden.

Life

I was in love with You. You were with me when I crawled, waltzed, cried. You brought me roses, helped tend my garden. You dried my tears when I spent prom night alone. You danced with me, hitchhiked across Europe, slept with me under the stars in Montana, looked closely at moose in Alaska, caught a muskie with Jerry in Wisconsin, climbed over ancient rock, gave counsel to struggling students, stood in front of the classroom, read passionate poetry.

With You I was always going to Colorado. Dreaming of old mines, lacy mountains, plank wooden sidewalks, wild Indian Paintbrush. Dreaming of plum skies and fresh campfires, thin smoke spiraling to the stars. Quarter horses, rattlesnakes, stones like salamanders, rough leather cowboy boots, caribou herds, mountain trails, sudden snowstorms. With You I used to glide in skis, zigzag down slopes in the ecstasy of youth. I was a bobbin unspooling, a spinning top—electric, on fire, as casual as a cowboy hat.

And now a pirate stalks me from behind, threatens the curve of my neck, settles for one breast, laughs at my scars, sits comfortably in a chair beside me. He takes You hostage, refusing to leave, silencing my tongue with terror . . .

> muted, I chase icy shadows
> dodge trees, ski
> out of bounds

PINK: Part II

Pink flamingo pretty ribbon bow girly girl perfume pink rose pale pink lipstick rose frosting cupcakes pink U.S. Strikes Syria ivory streamers cream white pure Mary virgin white noise cream puff white magic white hackers white witness white paper blank nothing yellow butterfly moth cocoon Cruise Missiles dandelion daffodil Yield sign light brilliant lightbulb crayon yield goldenrod gold nuggets gems ruby red rare steak garnet blood moon orange Gas Attacks sorbet sherbet orange vest hazard sign orange juice green sweater lawn grass stem leaf pine needle Billionaire Enters Governor's Race young forest young birds hummingbird blue ocean navy sky night black night close your eyes death pink palace Barbie with a mastectomy with a prosthesis with reconstruction Cop Recalls Being Shot pink haloes frilly dresses pink socks bubble gum barrettes Russia Invades Ukraine pink cheeks Trump's Border Wall rainbow fish scale ROYGBIV mirror reflection light sun rays tinted glasses Millions Die of COVID rose colored happiness.

After Reading Dorothy Parker

"It's brutal," my neighbor Gina says about the weather. Why did she even bother to stop by? Do I seem sick? She's wearing an ugly parka with some kind of faux fur. I need to write a poem. I don't tell her that, or that something has been bothering me. Every day, ideas. I write them down, shout them into my Siri.

"So how are you getting along?" she asks. "Your heat working OK?" Jesus. Doesn't she understand that I don't care? *Fine!* I practically shout. She has a mole on her left cheek that moves when she talks. The woodpeckers and nuthatches come to our feeder despite the early snow. Jerry is gone. I think he's getting the snowblower fixed. The branches are bare and black. I am writing these past few days. Wow. The cancer hasn't gotten me yet. I am writing.

"Do you need an extra blanket tonight? It's just so terribly cold." She is placating me now. I shake my head. The mole has a hair in it. Perhaps she should consider surgery. The squirrels are screeching; earlier, Canada geese flew high overhead, circling and squawking. Last night Jerry shoveled 25 feet around the perimeter of our driveway. We still don't know when the storm will end. Did I say the cancer hasn't metastasized yet?

"I swear," she says, "It's like I've gone into a deep freeze. Should we play Pinochle instead?" Why on earth would I want to play Pinochle? That's for old people. *No, no, no!* I reply. *No need to cancel plans just for the weather. Heavens! I'll adapt.* My former best friend is in India. She sent me a generic email, saying she is Happy. I hear the wind, but I don't feel it because I'm inside. My poor cat Mink. She also has cancer.

"Well," she twirls her keychain, "I didn't know if you were up for it." She turns her head so I can't see the mole. Instead, I notice her wiry hair is dirty. Despite the snow, the sun is shining through giant oak boughs. Winter is here. I'm not ready. *I'm fine,* I say. Did I mention my cancer is Stage 3?

"Josh said we would take a stroll on skis afterwards," she says, looking out the window. She wraps the ugly parka around her fat frame. *Go skiing?* I ask. *Oh, my. I think I've just come down with a terrible cold. I'll have to stay inside. DO go ahead without me. I wouldn't for the world want to stop you from going. Break a leg.* I can't even picture her on skis, with her fat stomach and all. And why would I want to go skiing?

"Well," she says, "if you're sure you're okay. I won't be long." She opens the door and steps outside. Finally! My Siri is yelling at me, gives me a list of places to go skiing. I shout into the phone, tell it to "Fuck Cancer!" Siri replies, "I don't know how to respond to that."

# III. Treatment

Chasing Bees

I was stung by a bee once while bicycling
along an old railroad trail in Wisconsin.
We had stopped to buy a soda. My arm
swelled like a pink balloon, but we pedaled
on through a quarter-mile tunnel.

"It's just like a bee sting," the radiologist
said, years later, holding up a long needle.
The tech moved the wand on my chest,
the needle pricked, and the bruising began.

It was sometime during this second biopsy
after the doctor stung my skin, guiding
the needle like a finger on a Ouija board
to collect tissue, when she answered a question,
stealing my breath before stapling four steel
pins deep into the apiary of my left breast.

"Most women don't die of breast cancer,"
she said, staring at the ultrasound screen.
She recommended a mastectomy, my milk
ducts contaminated, *invasive ductal carcinoma*
the official diagnosis. Perhaps at some point
I had been exposed to carcinogens, swarming
my body with polycyclic aromatic hydrocarbons,
hexagonal-shaped cells not unlike honeycomb.

And I couldn't stop thinking about the bees,
how they must feel during hive collapse. They
abandon their queen, the majority leaving behind
only a bit of food and a few other workers.

My grandfather minister raised bees. Church ladies
lined up every Sunday, waiting for a bee sting
that was supposed to cure their arthritic hands.

In my dreams I drown in honey, my body stung
and swollen as I swim in wound-healing liquid,
the queen raising me higher and higher—
no drones, no destroyed hives, no biopsies—
until all I see is light, flowers, wax and seeds—
my broken stinger trailing behind me.

Thoughts Before My Mastectomy

—*after Lawrence Ferlinghetti*

The anesthesiologist introduces himself,
bores his kind brown eyes into mine
as I lie on the hospital gurney.
I ask him when I will wake up.
He says he doesn't know.

I am waiting to wake up.

I am waiting for a new flower
to emerge, and I am waiting
to label that flower an orange lily.

I am waiting for the day
I will really enjoy fruit.

I am waiting for the moment
you come home from work
and I am waiting for the fresh earth
and clean rain to germinate that lily.

I am waiting in the day surgery room,
sprawled on an operating table.
I am waiting for someone to remove
this IV, to remove this breast, to shout,
"Hey! Your tumor is gone! Cancer has
finally, inevitably, irrevocably been
eradicated from your body!" But no!

I am waiting to fall off earth, to sail in space
and mingle with the planets. I am waiting
to see Mom and Dad again, to hold hands
with their spirits, to not wince at pain.

I am waiting for a new chance at life,
to see the sun transform our planet
into True Love, for light on our garden,

for a sprig of lily and fresh orange juice.
Yes! I am waiting for you and for the
operation, and I am waiting to thank

my surgeon and my anesthesiologist
1,000 different ways—all grateful,
beholden—for trying to save my life.

Radiation

In the waiting room, a 40ish woman with Judy Dench hair, me almost bald. Her hair just starting to come back. Mine a salt and pepper black / gray stubble, hers dark red. She is at the end of radiation treatment. She says it's not so bad. She says she bought an aloe plant instead of lotion. "An aloe plant?" I ask. "I am just putting lotion on it. Can't you just buy aloe lotion?" Nope, she says, an aloe plant. "Works wonders," she says. Then, suddenly, she blurts out, "Wanna see?" She rips open her robe to show me dark, blistered skin. I try not to blink or look disgusted. "I'm doing pretty good," she says. "Only two more to go, then the Boost." The Boost is an optional treatment given at the end of therapy to add an extra punch. I will get the Boost too. Six days of targeted radiation at the scar since it is most likely to see a recurrence. I'm not sure what to say. My skin only has a mild tan. "You know," she whispers, closing her robe. "People always say, 'You are so brave to battle Cancer, or to go through chemo.'" She shakes her head. "But it's not that. If they only knew we are desperate! We have no choice!" she says. "Angela?" the nurse calls. She gets up to go. "Well, I'm not burnt meat yet," she laughs, then frowns, leaning down to whisper, "I hope to God it's through."

> Beams of light
> pierce the chest wall—
> a forest of birches, charred.

Cancer, Part I

My body is an oil rig.
Inside flammable liquid
safe for now a protected
embryo until one cell
goes rogue one tire skids
and all raw goods and crude
tumble, spill onto concrete.

My lymph nodes are highways
of toxicity, my scars, railroad
tracks. My veins contain
fierce semis loaded with
germs and poison and fumes.
Their convoys are pink skin
beaten down by wave
after wave of radiation.

When I accelerate, drive blindly
towards the next infusion,
my port provides navigation
as I move past the intersection
of chemicals and confession.

I see my life like a freighter
and I pick up the CB radio,
wildly try to connect with
anybody with everybody

until I remember not to fill up
on the wrong kind of fuel,
but instead to lean closer
to Love and let the wind
whisper its prayer.

Resistance

Battle-ridden soaked deflated
knock-kneed and shaking
but not defeated
we grip pink bayonets
take refuge in our surgeon's artillery
take aim at each tumor's tank
bushwhack past diagnoses

until we lie on the battlefront
worn out by biopsies
by poisonous gases
chemo   radiation
when we see the enemy
we do not hide   but transform
serving as a spy for the cure

Despite the torture of hours
and guerilla infantry of chemical
poison to our bodies we lead
the resistance and work
to tackle these foreign invaders

what are we but lost
victims   searching
what are we
but mermaids missing
one or both breasts
long hair to cover
scars   and shame
as we attempt to perform
water ballet, synchronized
swimming, attempt to escape

the eternal nausea, fear
while our scaly
tails go *thwump, thwump*
keeping time with Persephone
and her descent.

Surfacing

Swimming through mud
breaststroke   sinking
further down the rabbit hole
pocketing bitter truths
like vitamins to be swallowed later
with rainwater, digging further and further
until the mind melts,
explodes.

In one big bang
I surface
and all the burning and puking and infusion
folds into the pudding of the planet
the midnight moon
shines down on diagnoses
my feet caked with pink slime.

Under the stars,
hair becomes linguini
organs   cottage cheese
mouth   a falling star
breasts   the Milky Way.

I breathe.

Pink Slime

—after Wilfred Owen

Bent double like pink peonies with ants
bald scarf-bedecked, or with cranial
prosthesis attached, we walk
arm in arm
a pink palisade of ladies
drunk from weeks of chemo
scarred we turn our backs
on blind oncologists
and towards the distant light
begin to see women counting
their lymph nodes, admiring
their tattooed nipples, lost bras
yet still they linger on, losing
eyelashes, eyebrows, pubic hair,
and like burgers they go double, single.

Alive! Quick, girls, apply the salve
to your burning skin. Fumble your
way to next month next year, but lo!
Someone has spotted another lump
five years past hysterical crazy
she gazes at the firing squad
only to sink slowly
into an ocean
of pink slime.

Echocardiogram

> *... how infinitely the heart expands*
> *to claim this world, blue vapor without end.*
> —Lisel Mueller

The technician has a soft Filipino accent.
He unties my gown, covers my chest
with a damp towel.

He takes pictures of my heart
shows me the dark screen
of my beating machine.

The U.S. Education system is ruined,
he says. *My kids are suffering.*
I've lost so much in the stock market.

I look at the ceiling while he probes
my left side with a magnetic wand.

The ultrasound screen beeps. He blinks.
All hospitals want techs with a university
degree. I only have an associate's
from a defunct school.

I don't want to think of all that could go
wrong. I like to think my heart is strong.

So many years ago, cancer strangled me
like vines. What can I say to convince
this man his suffering is fluid like a river?

*It's too expensive to go back to college.
And I have the beginnings of sciatica nerve.
Why do I have to work so hard to feed my family?*

My mother's heart did not stop on her deathbed for minutes. I don't tell him that it has taken me all my life to face fear. I can hear my mother's voice whispering, stronger than gravity.

I lean towards him and try to say the right thing.

Cancer, Part II

—a golden shovel poem after "old relative"
by Gwendolyn Brooks

He approached me like a lover after
the sweaty sun had set and the
moon rose with the stars, the swans in baths,
the deer hiding among trees, and
squirrels bedded down among the bowels
of black oak branches. I knew there was work
to do, but he was a charmer, not cruel but he
destroyed half my body while it was
blooming. I winked at the sky, but it was dead.

Our Lover

At the Infusion Center my last chemo ten days ago now I need a blood test. Suddenly I hear my name. "I met you at Wellness House! At the makeup class!" A pretty young woman is smiling, hair tucked under a gold mohair beret, her mascara accentuating large blue eyes. "Yes!" I say adjusting my coarse brown wig. She sits down, asks how I am doing. I don't tell her of my abusive lover my black eye, broken teeth, I am discrete, tell her I will get another mastectomy, ask about her surgery. "Tuesday," she says. "I just said, 'Take them both.'" I nod I don't tell her my body is a shipwreck, my scar rusted iron, my Lover has shaved my skin and left me with terror and silence. "My name is Margaret," she reminds me her eyes, her beautiful eyes brimming with watery happiness & hope & she is smiling I don't tell her, keep my thoughts to myself . . . she will find out . . . she has the same Lover I do and he is very, very tricky.

Metamorphosis

"Now approaching Hinsdale!!" the conductor calls.
A child cries, "Whoa! Look at those cars!"
I look out the window at the snow.

>*Take three deep breaths my OT had said*
>*massaging my arm to stimulate the lymph*
>*nodes decimated from surgery, radiation.*

Unlit streetlamps, kids unwrapping candy,
the crinkling of cellophane, red and green.
We go under a viaduct, a whistle blows.

>*Last year my husband wrapped my left arm*
>*tightly every night in gauze like a mummy.*

We race past rusted corrugated buildings,
barbed wire on a chain link fence.
Then the thunder of a freight train.

>*The OT showed me how to exercise my arm*
>*to move the lymph fluid out of my body.*

Green box cars give way to white,
gray piggybacks give way to steel,
give way to high rise brick condos,
give way to one eggshell blue building . . .

>*Today I received the All Clear. No*
>*lymphedema anymore. No swelling*
>*of the left arm or fingers.*

give way to magenta and white graffiti,
to circular tracks as the train leans
into the V-shaped lane and we
approach the silver skyline of Chicago.

> *Thoughts of cancer disappear as we move
> into a tunnel. I have become Phoenix,
> resurrected from my wounds.*

The Second Arrow

What has no shadow, has no strength to live.
—Czeslaw Milosz, "Faith."

"Choose any spot you like," my oncologist says. I pick an overstuffed Lazy-Boy next to an IV, park my bag full of books, then she leaves. Soon a nurse greets me, says she will be taking care of me for the next four hours. I touch the scar where my left breast used to be and try not to think of any upcoming cocktail treatments—chemotherapy, radiation, tamoxifen, with a splash of more surgery. I wish instead I could get drunk on real Russian vodka, wake up when it is all over to find it had only been a fraternity party.

I stare at the nurse's straw blonde hair damaged from years of dyeing and can't help but think of all the money I've put into my own hair—expensive cuts, keratin treatments, highlights. I am still getting used to the smooth dark synthetic locks and bangs of my "cranial prosthesis," trying not to laugh at how one of my favorite students said three times, in all seriousness and naivety, "I'm likin' the new hair, Ms. J."

The nurse dabs alcohol on my port, then sticks the needle into my skin. The first step is flushing the port, then I am given an hour's worth of anti-nausea medication, followed by the big Red Devil, Adriamycin. The nurse brings the bright cherry liquid in a syringe and injects it into my skin. Soon I will be peeing pink.

I first met my oncologist five years ago at a party at her house, a multimillion-dollar estate with swimming pool and tennis courts. The party was for her sister, a friend of mine; I remember a conversation in the kitchen about T.S. Eliot. The oncologist was clutching a wine glass, explaining how a group of doctors, including herself, had started a poetry club. I wondered how scientific people like doctors and engineers think, if they needed more poetry in their lives than most people.

After she discovers I like poetry, the chemo nurse tells me of her favorite poem, "The Hound of Heaven," an epic Christian ode about running away from a loving God. I look it up on my phone and read it. I want to discuss it, have a conversation about why the protagonist doesn't recognize God, but she just bends down and flushes my port again.

Weeks earlier my oncologist told me about her trip to Africa, about the lions she saw on her safari. That was after I learned my treatment would last not months, but years. I was assigned a navigating nurse to answer any questions I might have, but I sensed burnout as I caught her several times sitting by a large window of light. Other nurses, like Pam from the Philippines and Sue whose husband lives three states away, work to brighten my mood as they inject my body with drugs. A young nutritionist visits periodically to talk about what I should and should not eat.

But it is the chaplain whom I love. He is from Georgia and wears a suit. We talk about Flannery O'Connor and Mary Oliver. He likes British History while I prefer American. As we talk I feel myself transforming, as if someone is trying to help me carry some unbearably heavy stone. Then one day he tells me of the second arrow as I try not to think about what a woman said in a support group, how her port-a-cath leaked and all the veins on her right side lit up like a Christmas tree.

The first arrow is the suffering, the true suffering, he said, quoting the Buddhist mystic Thich Nhat Hanh. It comes from without and we have no control over it. The second arrow is how we hurt ourselves. It comes from within: criticism, worry, brooding, and depression. The chaplain told me not to listen to the second arrow, not to hurt myself. Yet I can't help but feel I have crossed a border, unwillingly been deported to another country. It is strange and foreign and I don't speak the language. I am always trying to get back to the Land of Before. The doctor is my coyote as I trespass the rocky desert under open sky, past barbed wire diagnoses and the Rio Grande, past nausea and fatigue and clumps of hair, past biopsies and bone scans, as I try to return home. In the end, I am alone.

IV. Recovery

Slumber

A quilt of snow covers your garden,
the stone goose is naked, gray, only
a thin line of frost ices the oak tree.
What will happen this spring?
Will the zinnias and celosia burst
like they did last year? Will you be
here, my dear? Will I? Will all the bright
colors—fuchsia, carmine, buttercup, ochre—
burst in an umbrella of joy, purple coneflowers,
black-eyed Susans, milkweed that attracts
monarchs, ruby-throated hummingbirds,
honeybees, butterfly bushes. All the gentle
creatures love what I love—your garden
now is sleeping. Shhh. Don't disrupt it.
Don't wake Sleeping Beauty until Mother
Nature is ready to kiss the Rose of Sharon,
the pastel tulips, lily of the valley, ferns,
hostas, now dormant, now waiting.

Descending

The stairs are steep, coated in snow.
I grip the railing. At each slow step,
my knees creak. Then an older man
greets me as he walks up the ice.
"You are a brave woman!" he exclaims,
his eyes smiling. How does he know?
Can he see under my winter parka?

A friend said three years ago, before
I started chemo, *You are so brave.*
I look beyond the man at the bleached
logs floating in the stream below,
at the bridge now broken that once
ferried hikers. I shiver, grip the railing,
continue my descent . . . one step at a time.

Sparrow

On my walk: a few butterflies two rabbits one tiny sparrow with a broken wing nudged out of its nest too soon now hopping landing on a hubcap I want to

save it like the robin eggs hatched outside our garage this spring . . . four hungry mouths wide open eyes closed not afraid of my camera until they opened their eyes I saw

the Mama nearby on a telephone wire, flying to the nest with a huge worm in her beak, attacking us if we got too close I wonder

if my odds are as good as these baby birds they say I have three out of four chances I will survive this cancer I notice only three robins are left now I wish

I could lounge all day in a nest with my beak open I wish my mother could attack cancer and keep it away I wonder

what happened to that sparrow I couldn't save.

March

brutally cold
the kind of wind that seeps
through your skin, unkind
as we wait for spring
not quite yet the cruelest
month. I walk across campus
hold a scarf to my face
hold together my life
as thoughts spin despite
the weather despite cancer
I am happy. I have the Coat
of Love swaddling my trauma.
Inside the office a warm cup
of coffee, paper to write
a poem, and a pen. I am ready
for the morning, and for the
mourning, should it come.

Amazons

I used to walk the Continental Divide high up
in the Rockies, my companions Dall sheep
and aspen, lichen, forget-me-nots, lime green
moss growing on large boulders. So long ago

I embraced the sky as I hiked tundra and valleys.
To look at the mountains set me free. I trekked,
ambled, climbed, camped. I aimed to go far away
from civilization, found others along the way.

Now, post-surgery, my scars permanently sewn
on my chest, I don't hike the Continental Divide
anymore. I don't stop to smell lavender, thistle,
aster or Indian Paintbrush. Instead, I dream

of fourth-century BC Scythian women who rode
horses into battle. What spears! What iron daggers!
What perfect quivers and bronze-tipped arrows!
Oh! The perfection of a Scythian bow—small, powerful.

Amazon Sisters, what gifts did you give Penthesilea,
your queen? What wounds did you procure? You
smoked pot, got tattooed. You were buried maimed,
scarred, some with legs akimbo like an isosceles

triangle, as if you were still riding. Next to you lay
horse bones and tackle. I wonder if I could make
a spear out of lodgepole pine, deciduous leaves,
Rocky Mountain maple, fireweed and harebell.

Maybe I should pray to Cybele, goddess of the moon, like the Amazons did, ask her to carve a path of light to protect Pink Sisters before they go to battle, before they become warriors and go into the dark night.

Dance of the Adders

Two male adders rise, side by side,
black as night, intertwined in a dance.
I watch them fight over me,
wrestling in the moonlight.

Of the twin vipers, Cancer is one.
The other, my faith in good health.
Which will be my Lover? Their dark
scales gleam, giving no answer
as they coil, belly to belly.

Thick-bodied, with hinged fangs,
adders inject venom into their prey.
The forked tongue strikes, the head
hisses and lunges. If I fought an adder,

I would strike from behind, kill him
as I have destroyed my tumor, flay
his carcass so it sheds like a dead husk.
I could disguise my pheromones so he

wouldn't want to mate, make my back
the color of chameleons, slide down a black
branch, embracing violence to my body,
scarred as it is, grateful as I have become.

Spuds

Yesterday was National Potato Chip Day. I received an email from a women's magazine with all kinds of potato chip recipes. Who knew the combination of salt and grease could be so good? So many times I've indulged: plain, malt vinegar, sour cream and onion . . . my brother's special potato casserole recipe . . . spuds, sour cream, and lots and lots of potato chips. A secret recipe he doesn't share with anyone. In the olden days, Before Cancer (BC), I could splurge on kettle potato chips and not think of anything except joy, and perhaps occasionally, calories. Now, whatever I eat is a matter of survival. The stakes are higher, and I calculate much more than fat. I must choose wisely. Sadly, potato chips are not on the smart choice list. Days pass with no spuds, whether mashed, scalloped, fried, baked or chips. Only beets, kale, tomatoes, tofu, and fruit. Woefully, I choose.

She Says Blue Looks Good on Me

As I sit across from her at Panera
measuring her huge brown eyes,

my brief cami shows some cleavage,
despite only one breast and a scar.

She says I look great, looking sideways
at the auburn wig. I get into my car,

merge with traffic, wait to shift gears
and plow on, like a true soldier.

Tai Chi

To hold the world between your palms
to push it up and over your head
then side to side, caressing it
like an ancient Greek statue
of a naked man. I hold this globe
carry it close to my flat chest
it becomes my Chi, the life force
flowing in and out of me.

The teacher tells us to imagine
we are holding a small ball.
I cup my hands and the circle
becomes an orb of fire.
I push it left and right
it contains the ocean,
waves in slow motion.

The strangers next to me all
have cancer. The ball becomes
a balloon, lifting each tumor outside
our bodies, into the air where
the wind takes it to a place of despair,
where it can never escape or recur.

Later the ball surfaces again when
I lie next to you. It becomes
a tulip bulb, a red geranium
in a broken pot, a nasturtium
in full bloom outside our window.

Like the way you reel in your pike,
the river's surface blue and full of light,
the dancing glitter in celestial eyes,
the moon recalling the ghost of night,

I hold your soul close.

Moon Walk

I walked to the lake tonight,
dark boughs fanned the light
of the moon as I hiked the scree
to see the water. Could only imagine
what lay underneath—fresh-faced bluegill
who in day shimmer with soft-scale
xylophone iridescence. I closed my eyes,
woke to loose threads spinning wildly
from my mind like Medusa's snakes, they
wove and unraveled as I sat moored
on the bank, broken metamorphic rocks
combined with worn-soft sedimentary stones.
I waited for courage to claim this dark place.
I had traveled there, descended not to Hades,
but to the possibility of cancer's recurrence.
Maybe if I waited long enough I would find
agates, geodes, escape this nightmare
by panning for gold. The moon grinned at me
deliriously. I stood up to leave, felt comfort
when I finally came home, the front light shining
on your outrageous wildflower garden. I embraced
the sunflowers, purple coneflowers, black-eyed
Susans, milkweed. I smelled the rose petals. Tomorrow
the sun will chase away the moon, and there will be
monarchs and hummingbirds, rubies and diamonds.

V. Spirit

The Healer

Celestial light from the universe shines
through her skeletal eyes, full
of Day of the Dead fruit, sugar
candy, offerings and sacrifices
to lithe spirits who follow her,
who linger like guardian angels.

And I am hurting. I need a curandera
fresh from the dry desert to kill my scorpions
to feed me tortilla soup, avocado, and tamales
made of corn that the *abuelas* spent two days
mashing and wrapping with husks.

I tell her of a painting I saw once
of a dark peasant woman with one
giant black breast that seemed to blend
with the rolling hills of Brazil.

She carefully lifts my veil of stars
looks straight into my eyes, clasps
her hands like the Virgin Mary.
Despite her Catholic gaze I cannot
think of prayer. I go to a different
mass, my holy communion a wish bone
caught in my throat, while all the
madres, padres, hermanos y hermanas,
circle round her like gentle cherubs.

But she knows my secrets, does
what all good healers do—peeks into
the horror to pluck out the plum of suffering,
holds it up to the light so it transforms
from a heavy piece of rotten fruit
into a fawn with fragile shoulders.

I watch as it stumbles away and grows wings.
I am as light as air.

Last of the Seers

—on viewing an exhibit of photos of the Sistine Chapel

Of all the paintings Michelangelo
created for the Sistine Chapel,
none move me like this woman.

Not Eve reaching for the apple
from a lifelike serpent, nor the lightning
touch of God in the Creation of Adam.

She is wearing a long strapless orange dress,
this Libyan Sibyl, the last of the seers created
on the north side of the chapel's fresco.

I, too, wore a strapless dress 20 years ago
on my wedding day. But compared to her,
my arms and neck are weak, undeveloped.

She is lifting behind her a huge book.
She looks backwards over her powerful
shoulder, while gazing in another direction.

Will she reach into her giant book to proclaim
an oracle? I am praying to this erudite woman
to divine my future, to say if I will survive cancer.

Soon I will weep like Jeremiah with his long white
beard, bright orange cloak. Perhaps it will be for joy,
like David upon slaying Goliath. Or will it be because

of my expulsion from Paradise? Will I be one of the chosen?
Or instead condemned to private darkness, the shadow side
of God's miraculous separation of Light from Dark.

Samskaras

All our samskaras—the vast ocean
underneath each person—we see
only the tip, the imprint left behind.

And now, the first time I've
made it through one whole day
without thinking about it. Instead,
only warm, positive thoughts,
full of poetry, friendship and love.

Watched a red-bellied woodpecker peck
at seeds. Pet my two cats. Tomorrow,
the gaping dark locks of my wig, but
it's OK. Today I sped down the highway
in the dark, sang with the radio.

All the while with no bone in my throat.
Only an impression of joy, an island of hope.

Wind Warrior

Created from evolution, with the help
of wind, stone, and the breath of the Beloved,

I willed my first step in an angel's image,
sanded my samskaras from thousands of years,

prayed to stay awake, to be a warrior.
You don't have to like me. You don't

even have to be like me. Created from
the ghost of my tumor, from spirit consciousness,

I sing inside to the goldfinches surrounded
by sacred ochre sky. With new wings broken

in all the important places, I cannot fly, yet still
I glide, feet no longer anchored in mud, but free,

my soles now breathing Amarillo air. I am grateful
for each day, each hour, each moment. Should I

fall I know my sisters will gently kiss my blue
shoulders, lift the veil separating me from You.

Blood Falls

The red-brown Blood Falls in Antarctica
are named for their unusual color.
—from National Geographic

In my nightmare I walk on a lunar landscape
somewhere in the depths of Antarctica.
Below lies a two-million-year-old river
sealed like a cordoned-off crime scene
from any form of life, save bacteria,
which has gorged on sulfate for eons.

Brackish, dark-red water three times
as salty as the sea burbles as if from
some unseen wound. I scoop up
handfuls of the gruesome liquid.

I am not asking for millions of years,
the age of this subglacial reservoir.
A decade or more would satisfy me.

Water stains my fingers like a murder
weapon as rime forms on my skin,
hiding a silent tumor. Though I know
I can't live without oxygen, in my
dreams I baptize myself with the brine
of Blood Falls, dive into its benthic

depths, cleanse my bones, surface
to return to the ice, to the stark
pilgrimage where I began.

My Wound

Hungarians call it seb (*sheb*),
this thin frown embedded
on my chest, left behind
after three surgeries.

It leaks when angered,
shoots forth blood, gushes
fluid like a waterfall.

Rooted in radiated skin
that is bronze, punctured,
stretched taut as clinging
cellophane. When I pull
the bandage, the broken
cut cries, oozes, leaving
behind soiled gauze.

My wound leans to the left
of my chest, next to my heart
like a cherry blossom. So slow
to heal, it embodies all the bad
I've done. But when mended,

my scar redeems me, carves
a path across dark skin like
the wrought iron and stone
Széchenyi Chain Bridge
in Budapest, lighting up
the oily Danube at night.

Circles

Everything emanates
from the center
and if the center is joy
all the spokes shoot
a river of light
into the sea
but if the core is pain
suffering waves
crash onto sand.

And the pain is pummeled
and polished
like a piece of dirt
in an oyster
becomes a pearl,
a scar
a beautiful, shiny scar.

Modlitwa*

We have a soul at times. No one's got it non-stop.
—Wislawa Szymborska

A Great Blue Heron
fishes in the forested canal
balancing on one stick leg
next to painted turtles
sunning on logs as I
bicycle along.

      pedaling faster . . .
      dreams fly by
      with the leaves

Then hundreds march toward me
chanting Polish, *Kristos,* a boy in front
bearing a giant Cross, followed by
the priest. I begin sweating, try
to plow through, but the thick
crowd does not budge.

Their chorus becomes a dirge.
I am thrown sideways as wild
thorns pierce my shorts, T-shirt.
Blocked by the seekers, I turn back.
Later, a woman from the pilgrimage
vows to pray for me. I thank her,
remove a tiny thorn from my hair.

*Polish for "prayer"

Prayer

> *They don't seem to believe in their happiness,*
> *And their song mingles with the moonlight,*
> *With the sad and beautiful moonlight,*
> *Which makes the birds in the trees dream*
> *And sob with ecstasy the water streams*
>   —Paul Verlaine, "Clair de Lune"

Too many thoughts as I walk the school halls.
A student on probation. My husband's vertigo.
A trip to the vet to put down our blind cat.
My cancer. What's for dinner tonight—ham?

Sound interrupts my world. Some kid
on the piano, Debussy's "Clair de Lune."
I stop, transfixed, the melody like a Muslim
call to prayer, the muezzin beckoning me
to abandon what I am doing and follow
the song straight to a long-ago memory.

I am back in Istanbul, drinking hot apple tea,
haggling over a Turkish carpet. A horse-drawn
carriage maneuvers traffic, and the minaret
of the Blue Mosque shimmers in haze.
Soon the sun will be setting, replaced
by the moon, perhaps a blue moon.

Before traveling, before I became a teacher,
I, too, used to play "Clair de Lune," dreaming
of moonlight on water as I fingered the notes.
The arpeggios helped me forget my worries.

I want to stand here and linger, listen to this
student's music, but people might think it strange.
Besides, I have places to go. I have spent my time
dreaming. Soon, I will be sobbing with ecstasy.

The Other Garden: A Haibun

Gravel driveways parched lawns Starbucks wrappers Realtor signs brick bungalows. Black ants carrying their dead, sidewalk weeds, peeling post office boxes, a barking pug. Each day on my walk I pass the garden, nestled in front of his vine-choked house. No lawn, only flowers, bushes, trees, ornate ceramic bird houses, gurgling stone water fountains, tiny orange marigolds, purple petunias, phlox. As I circle, the skunk smell of marijuana, moths hovering instead of monarchs.

> thirsty roots
> nourished by light
> despite tumor

Each time I walk by I see more—worn Winnie-the-Pooh stuffed animals, disheveled dolls, faded stuffed ladybugs, deflated beach balls, a ceramic goose—gifts from friends, family. Today a purple butterfly bush and a potted pink geranium.

> sunflowers bloom in a secret garden
> mind opens bravely to the bees

Freedom

I said *libre*. She argued, said the Latin word is *gratis*. There is a difference. *Libre* is more French. It is more a feeling. *Gratis* means you get something for free. You didn't earn it. I take a walk every day for free. My Spanish lessons are free. Are the best things in life really free?

>my *esprit-de-corps* life
>just one crooked seed away
>from catastrophe

I walk past hydrangeas, ferns, hostas, zinnias, and sunflowers. My cancer is free. The gardener also has a fountain and a large mirror.

>gratitude
>a free gift if we look
>hard enough

VI. Survival

Flight

We take off, fly higher above the stricken highways,
ribbons of construction, stitches of madness, toxic
routes of meaninglessness. What would Camus
think? Has he ever flown in a plane? I am like
Siddhartha living through all the cycles of life.
I have come full circle, the roads I travel again
and again, each time with new eyes until it seems
I have come to the end of my dream. This airplane

is taking me to the next stage of life, my awareness
always conscious of what I have learned, what I
can impart to others. The grass and trees blend
with the haze of the clouds. Light shines on rooftops,
squares and squares of fields. No flowers from here.
Just altitude, depth, height and perspective.
The garden is below but I cannot see it.
My eyes follow the longest road that cuts
through prairie. Soon even that will disappear.

The Language of Cancer

I

Before my teenage sister got bone cancer
we would listen to her play Jim Croce,
Scott Joplin, Neil Diamond, John Denver.
After the diagnosis, she continued to play,
leaning into the piano keys and pumping
the damper pedal with her good leg.

When she was dying, sometimes I would
sit on the floor behind our living room couch
and look out a window at the stars. I didn't
know then how to pray. I would spend
recess at school throwing a red rubber
ball against a brick wall, over and over again.

The day my sister died, my father hung up
the phone with the doctor who told him
they had turned off my sister's life support.
He shook his head like a weary mule
too tired to pull its load. I wish I had
taken him up in my arms so that we
both could sob on each other's shoulders.
Instead, I ran outside to play with Johnny B.

It was autumn and the leaves were changing.
I wish I could say I talked to Johnny about cancer.
Instead, we climbed our tree house, shot rocks
from homemade slingshots onto neighbors' lawns.
When his mother asked me how Debbie was doing,
I looked down at my 8-year-old hands, squinted
my eyes and said nothing. Silence was an old friend.

My other sister, on hearing the news, left the house
carrying a bottle of Woolite. She marched one long
block to a long-time friend of the family who had asked
to borrow the detergent. The Woolite bottle had no cap.

II

Creole is an oral language that is a serenade
when spoken aloud, with a lilting melody that loses
its power once written down. The syntax becomes
tortured and dies. Like Latin, it loses its life.
I've never spoken Creole or heard it, but I imagine
it is like music. You become alive when playing
the piano or guitar. The melody lifts spirits,
the songs connect hearts. But if you just look
at the black notes on the page, they mean nothing.

As the years passed I learned all of the songs
Debbie played. I practiced every day, and sometimes
my parents would ask me to play for dinner guests.
Full of liquor, tears streaming down his face, my father
remembered his oldest daughter through my music.
The dinner guests listened patiently, picking
at their Steak Diane and sipping their Chianti.

III

More than forty years later, my wig safely stowed
in the attic, my new hair, chemo-soaked, lies in tight
curls against my scalp. I swallow pills each morning
and night, a scar emblazoned on my chest like radiated
kryptonite, a stoic reminder of all the Amazon women
before me, survivors who cauterized their right breast
to better fit their bow and arrow, or so the legend goes.

I understand a new language. But like written Creole,
cancer's vocabulary stays buried with the memory
of all the casseroles the neighborhood ladies kindly
made so long ago for our family. A tricky vernacular,
fear keeps me from blurting out my secret. Like my sister,
I wear a prosthesis, stand strong and tall, but when I play
"Annie's Song" or "The Entertainer," the dead language
comes to life, and I join the ghosts who wake up and sing.

Refuge

—at the Willowbrook Wildlife Center

Tell me what you did
pretty red fox
before someone found you
orphaned, deaf, before
you were adopted
by Mrs. Carrion's First Grade
at Walt Whitman Elementary School.

You rest in your cage,
like all the injured birds here—
red-shouldered hawk, great-horned
owl, barred owl, common sparrow—
blind, fractured, broken with concussion.
What did you do before someone
brought you to this suburban oasis?

Red fox, what are we to do?
I have only my scarred and bruised body,
my wounds still fresh, my mouth dry.

I cannot fly, but like the cardinal,
I can sing. I come before you
an injured thing.

How to Kill Cancer

1. Be ready to do battle.
2. Always be on guard.
3. Defend your fortress.
4. Don't let anything seep through your feathers.
5. Lean into the wind, and, if possible, unburden your wings.
6. Remember you were blue sky once, floating in yolk until a thin line cracked, and Hell broke.
7. You almost suffocated from a dark center where cancer feasted on cells, then you emerged from the nest whole and changed, watching a butterfly sail towards a purple coneflower.
8. Your mother taught you well. Spear your enemy. You know the one, the jet-black hawk that destroys everything.
9. Set out some bait.
10. Sharpen your beak.
11. Kill with kindness.
12. Try any kind of treatment.
13. When you do kill, turn your prey round and round until you find its heart, dip it in salt, eat hungrily. It tastes better than a worm.
14. Above all, do not give in to sad silence, apathy, or self-pity, the chorus of cardinals or wrens.
15. Fly, if possible, to your own sounds of laughter. Watch as lightning bugs rise slowly, turning on and off, on and off, leaving behind a bright vapor of light. Your Hope.

Rowing

—after Pablo Neruda

It so happens I am sick of being a woman.
I drive slowly, afraid of road rage,
monsters with misogynist feet.

The smell of department store shadows
makes me grow toe fungus, the touch
of silk and Styrofoam and vanity
unhinges me.

It would be marvelous
to terrify a librarian with my single
mastectomy, to grow eyes
where a nipple used to protrude,
to let loose the curls of my
chemo-soaked hair
to stare at giant ghosts
with the air of recurrence.

I don't want to wait for D-Day,
insecure, hovering in my corner,
eating huckleberry pie and pot roast,
going down, down into the guts
of earth's womb. I don't want
to mingle with corpses.

But rather, I want to face Monday,
emerge at dawn and row myself
toward a gray angel, a psychedelic
clock—to motor gracefully
on a lake of a billion marbles
and feel the sacred ground
of survivorship as I unburden
my parachute.

On Our 20th Wedding Anniversary

—a FANBOYS poem*

For it was a Sunday long ago
when the small group of guests
gathered for our union.

And now after hundreds of hikes,
scores of fishing trips, and one cancer,
we haven't come undone.

Nor have we any desire to part,
despite thinning hair, radiated skin,
scars that ache, and a mortgage.

But before our parents lost their language,
before we sat on the porch of our current house,
we found new love, renewed our vows.

Or perhaps it was before the Rose of Sharon
bloomed that we ever imagined a gentle kiss
could stop our young knees from shaking.

Yet twenty years later, I have your name
tattooed on my heart as one by one
we connect the dots in a river of music.

So our lives teem with song, fast and fluid.
Each day you bait your hook, the Rose
of Sharon shakes its pink petals on my chest.

For what you catch is what I crave,
And what you sing is what we celebrate.
Nor do we need a hefty net of jazz,
But bank only on a symphony of promise,
Or perhaps an orchestra of potential that
Yet tethers our twin melodies together.
So we reel in new laughter each day.

*FANBOYS is an acronym used by English teachers around the world. It stands for the six coordinating conjunctions for, and, nor, but, or, yet, so. This poem uses all of these conjunctions in order.

Corn Maze

My husband likes to bushwhack
splitting branches, stepping over weeds,
ivy, dead logs, mud. Once, I followed.
Got stuck at the creek, couldn't cross
without falling. We turned back.
The fear of getting lost stopped
me from going again.

I like a path paved in tar or concrete,
walking where I know the end result.
No pebbles slide under my toes.
The unknown seems so knowable,
the path doesn't change, just
the clouds and the seasons
the people and the dogs.

I've never been to a corn maze, never
tried to shimmy my way out of a puzzle,
except in my mind, which could be worse,
depending. Maybe cancer is like that.
A big bardo, a Tibetan corn maze
that you never quite can get through,
but you try and try. I refuse to sit down,

will walk my way out of the labyrinth,
to find the sunset that inevitably follows
a sunrise, the death that follows birth,
the departure that echoes each arrival,
cutting my arms on each stalk and tassel.

Sonography of a Survivor

*so·nog·ra·phy (noun)—the analysis of sound using an instrument
that produces a graphical representation of its component frequencies*

She dials my ribs,
full of beautiful bones with no metastasis, yet.

> *Radiation, Adriamycin, Taxol, echocardiogram with
> strain, bald, scarf, wig, no hair on arms, legs.
> Double mastectomy, reconstruction, scars, saline,
> prosthetic, sparse eyebrows and pubic hair. Achy
> knees, numb under left arm.*

One year taken out of my life.

She dials my abdomen, full of bacteria,
beautiful bones with no metastasis—yet.

Migrating through the dark with sound,
the sonography of the possible map of my cure.

But there is no map, there is no cure,
just the chanting of my mantra:

That which doesn't kill you makes you stronger.

Dive into the dark world of spirit and the unknown.
Things change as you fall farther, where mermaids
have jumped, and sirens sing with broken bodies.

She dials my chest, muscles and beautiful bones,
with no metastasis—yet.

My hands.
My bones.
My scars.
My skull.
My organs.
My blood.

That which doesn't murder you, makes you grow.

My hands, micro-pathways to the stars,
pumping and pushing. My bones,
skeletons of sadness. My heart,
muscle of strength.

She dials my abdomen, dome-shaped,
my beautiful bones with no metastasis—yet.

A murky, gray moonscape on the dark screen.

My twin scars, one sits on radiated skin,
the other, a semi-frown, matches,
both laced in stitches. If they could talk,
they'd form a community of gangsters,
barroom bouncers who have fought
off infection and disease.

I have to do this. I have no choice.

What does a sonographer see
when she scans my skull?
A brain full of neurons,
intellect echoing madness,
leaps of intuition, a vast bank
full of prayer and insight?

Or just a bald head?

Numb under my left arm
like I was numb for one whole year.
Lost, one whole year.

There is the abdomen, full of bacteria,
beautiful bones with no metastasis—yet.

Radiologists translate sound waves,
echoes that bruise off body tissues,
organs making colorful images
on a screen that bursts and pops
with rainbow neurons and synapses.

That which provides no joy, produces poison.

Like a whale uses echolocation
in the deep to find prey, sonography
tracks each nodule on my chest,
heart, cervix, each reflection
and retraction of sound. The strength
of the echo, the map of my cure,
migrating through the dark cave,
where blood and muscle gel.

My blood a river of sweetness,
a myopia of mad energy,
furtive, feckless, but not free.

A sonographer dials my body.
What does she see?
My neck—firm lymph nodes
like a necklace, like licorice,
no toxic clavicle—yet.

My heart beats slow due to chemo,
tries to catch up—pure, exhausted,
it churns out anemic blood.

My bones, my beautiful bones,
strong with no metastasis—yet.

The only way to live with cancer . . .

My arms—strong from hugging.
My legs—propped when I am tired.
My chest—left side—burnt skin like tough
meat or shoe tongues, numb under the arm.

My scars red and swollen. My hair—
sparse eyebrows, pubic, leg, underarm.
My blood—full of Red Devil chemo, toxic
corpuscles, greedy river of poison.

My organs—fatty liver that fights every day.
Still fighting, brain still pumping, heart still
distilling blood, like fire sterilizes knives.

. . . is to practice joy . . .

My hair soaked by moist earth. My skin
hydrated with holy water. My breath
a blessing of air.

Not Alone

—with a line from Claude McKay's "If We Must Die"

If we must die, let it not be alone,
clothed in a hospital gown.
Surgical, clinical, urine-soaked and cold,
eyelids veiled and drowned.

If we must die, let us surrender to pink,
friend-filled, sighing to sisters.
Giddy and fierce, we won't stop to think
what could come *after,* thunderous twisters.

Let us rejoice in each hour and day—
each moment, each second, each year.
Not worry about how long life may take,
warm hugs instead of fear.

As women we'll face the common foe,
turn to the light when it's time to go.

To the 800,000 DACA Children,
from One Cancer Survivor

You can't remember your native land, can't recall
details of the crossing, but you sense hot air blowing
like an approaching hurricane, threatening
to uproot all of your sisters and brothers.

And if my wish for you has any power at all
so dirty politics will remain a lost memory,
and you will never have to bow again
to the scary Cerberus of silence, or whisper
a fervid prayer in each fear-packed moment.

My friends, you are soldiers and don't even know it.
Be like Perseus and slay the shadows of apathy
hovering in their caves. Throw Medusa's head
at the Department of Homeland Security. Don't
be afraid of senators grinning like jack-o-lanterns.
Lean instead toward the Day of the Dead, toward
the sugared skulls who seek to save your future
with placards and protests, who seek to spread justice
with hot churros and coffee. I say this to you as one

who has survived Cancer, that you, too, will outlive
this drama. I pray you will understand that each day
is a gift, a loan from the bank of time, that for every
pore of skin on your tired body, somebody also has
suffered a struggle, a thirst, a hunger, even a death.

You should know by now that, like all who persevere,
you are warriors, and even though you carry no
weapons you bear gifts of wisdom and dahlias.

Let the moon guide you. Let its light whisper past your fear and envelope you in the ghosts of your ancestors. Let tonight breathe wildly, not frightened like a rabbit, but stalwart as a coyote or wolf.

Open your history books and read with me. Study the Revolutionary War. Let Benjamin Franklin's famous words roll off your tongue, "Resistance to tyranny is obedience to God."

Veteran's Day

He said he had shrapnel in both shoulders,
that they had to do surgery on his back,
shoulders & eyes. Twenty years in the Army.
"It was harder to get out than to enlist,"
he said. Transferred to multiple hospitals,
he is now studying to be a nurse.

I can't help but wonder if he feels
as maimed as I do—both breasts gone,
one side radiated, huge scars across
my chest. I wonder silently about
his scars as I tell him he looks great.
"No one would know by looking at you."

I imagine us dancing, him leading me
in a slow waltz, cocking his head back
in a romantic gesture as he smiles and winks.

And suddenly I am 22 again, and I suppose
he is 25, and none of this ever happened.

My chest isn't radiated, skin a permanent
bronze, tough as shoe tongues.
He was not stationed across the world,
never a lifer who lost his identity.

I didn't lose all my hair, wear
the Michelle wig for almost a year.

No multiple surgeries on his shoulders, eyes.
His back, perfect. No invisible scars either.

Was I nauseous from chemo? I can't recall.
I only want to plead, *Make me feel beautiful again.*

No longer is he the scarecrow who lost all his hay.
In my mind I hear him say, *Put me back together again.*

Soldier at College

Dark hair, tan pockmarked skin, full mouth set in a tight smile. Before me, his simple GI bill. "I want to major in Biochemistry," he says. "I think I want to do experiments with plants so I can heal people." I adjust my wig. "Do you have any experience with plants?" I ask. "I mean, are you a Green Thumb?"

"No, ma'am." He leans down, shakes his head, then tells me of a time in Afghanistan when he used an aloe vera plant to heal second-degree burns. "I was just riding the CTA yesterday with a bunch of scientists. They were all going up north to study plants and herbs. And I thought, 'I could do that. I want to do that.'" He fidgets, stares at my computer, notices a picture I had forgotten I still had on the desktop. "Who's that?" he asks.

I grimace, not wanting to look at the picture of my bald head with a stubble of gray hair. I change the subject, purposely avoiding his eyes. I look up in one brief moment and see his kind eyes targeting mine.

"I took marksmanship classes, and courses on explosives," he said. "It's not the same thing as Chemistry."

I make a note to myself to be more careful with my photos. There are many ways we go to war, I think, and many ways we return.

VII. After

April in Garden of the Gods

Sunlight on sandstone as we make
our ascent to Camel Rock, leaving behind
purple redbuds that adorn the road.
Wildflowers have already burst into bloom—
Bluebell, Trillium, Mayapple, Arrowwood,
Dutchman's Breeches, Butterweed.

Atop the ancient hill, with its skyscraper boulders
and spring green trees, the violent remains
of a Cooper's Hawk encounter with a pigeon.
We wait for the sun to set surrounded by youth
who are on both sides of us, enjoying the rocks
without alcohol yet. Just days ago we slid through
Fat Man's Squeeze, where lovers have carved their
initials into rock for decades, then stumbled upon
a family cemetery tucked behind a one-room chapel.

I want to stay here and admire the blue and pink
of this day, knowing later we will warm ourselves
in a hot tub, settle on the stars, and you will kiss me
despite scars on my chest as we sing with the frogs
drenched in satin moonlight in back of our cabin.
Think. Just this morning I saw two newts on a trail.
And last night you pulled me outside to hear the owls.

At the Plaza del Carmen in Madrid

—with references to "Songs" by Frederico Garcia Lorca

The taxi drivers know this city by its plazas.
They measure distance not in kilometers,
but by cobblestone bricks, Hapsburg kings
and Bourbon queens. They tear through
Madrid with blood in their hearts, fuming
the air as tourist money pours into the city.

And I am walking with olives in my pocket,
dreaming about princes and Cordova.

Hundreds of years ago, the plazas were
a meeting place for *auto de fé,* the burning
of the body during the Spanish Inquisition.

So many paintings of martyred, tortured
saints line the Museo del Prada:
The Crucified Christ,
The Burial of Saint Sebastian,
The Martyrdom of Saint Agnes.

I think of Lorca, his books burned in Granada's
Plaza del Carmen, all banned in Franco's Spain.

Lorca wrote about Cordova, *far and lonely,*
before Franco's soldiers battered his body
with rifle butts, then riddled it with bullets.
To this day nobody knows where his remains lie.

So many pigeons line this plaza, strutting
like common peasants, pecking at bread,
pulling at crumbs from foreigners.

And death is watching for me.
Estoy llorando para ti, Frederico.
Like you, I'll never reach Cordova.

The Power of Pink

Watch out, Superman! We grab your back,
pump it up, surpass even Wonder Woman.
We bustle, radiate, swallow, inject, withstand, kick!
Every day, the faded ache, the pale pastel hue,
the stain of cancer worn like a badge.
We taste scared, pull apart when alone,
remain armed when combined, stay awake,
gorge on pink party cake.

Don't ask where we've been. We lift,
roar, dance, smack, punch, shout, fling!
We walk with our sisters on a faraway beach,
eat sponges with the endangered Hawksbill Turtle,
whose back keeps changing colors, whose flesh is toxic.

Don't try to catch us. Don't attempt to keep up.
We swim in coral reefs, emerge only to pledge
the pinky promise to each other
that should a second tumor appear—
a shark or Portuguese Man O'War—
we will circle closer, make spears
out of conch shells and halibut bones,
set well-placed nets across the jetty
then follow other mermaids out to sea.

Notes

Foreword:

"Chapel of Saint Petka in Belgrade." *Wikipedia.* Accessed 20 January 2025.

"Lives of the Saints—Martyr Parasceva and St. Petka-Paraskeva of Serbia." Orthodox America. *The Archives of Orthodox America.* This article details the life of St. Petka, and explains that those who prayed to her were "healed by various diseases and the blind received their sight." In addition, water from the St. Petka's spring in Belgrade was supposed to have cured many.

Ovid. *Metamorphoses.* Book III, line 425. 8th-century Roman poem. Qtd. in "How I Found an Unexpected Link Between Joy and Cancer." Living Well—BezzyBC. Caroline Johnson, author. Online. 16 Sept. 2024. Accessed 19 Jan. 2025.

Murakami, Haruki. *Novelist as a Vocation.* Trans. from the Japanese by Philip Gabriel and Ted Goossen. New York: Alfred A. Knopf, 2022. Page 125.

The Good Wolf Concept. A Cherokee parable paraphrased from "The One You Feed." Web. oneyoufeed.net/about-the-parable/ Qtd. in "How I Found an Unexpected Link Between Joy and Cancer." Living Well—BezzyBC. Caroline Johnson, author. Online. 16 Sept. 2024. Accessed 19 Jan. 2025.

Various excerpts from two online articles, "How I Found an Unexpected Link Between Joy and Cancer" and "My Travel Diary: Visiting Serbia and Croatia with Breast Cancer," both written by Caroline Johnson and shared with permission from bezzybc.com.

Poems:

"Mermaid in the Garden" epigraph taken from Linda Pastan's poem, "Purple," published in *Traveling Light.*

"The Last Toy"—The last stanza alludes to two poems, "How Do I Love Thee?" by Victorian poet Elizabeth Barrett Browning, and "The Good-Morrow" by 16th-century metaphysical poet John Donne.

"Driving Through the Dark" epigraph taken from Linda Pastan's poem, "Voices," published in *Carnival Evening.*

"PINK: Part II"—Portions inspired by newspaper headlines, especially from *The Chicago Tribune.*

"After Reading Dorothy Parker." Dorothy Parker (1893–1967) was an American poet and writer known for her sarcastic and caustic wit.

"Thoughts Before My Mastectomy" inspired by Lawrence Ferlinghetti's poem "I Am Waiting." Originally printed in *A Coney Island of the Mind,* 1950.

Both "Resistance" and "Pink Slime" allude to WWI poet Wilfred Owen's poem, "Dulce et Decorum Est," and compare cancer to war. The ending of "Resistance" refers to the story of the Greek goddess Persephone, who was said to descend to the underworld six months out of the year after she was abducted by Hades to be his bride.

"Echocardiogram"—the epigraph is from Lisel Mueller's poem, "Monet Refuses the Operation."

"Cancer, Part II" is a golden shovel poem inspired by a line from the poem "old relative" by Gwendolyn Brooks, "After the baths and bowel-work, he was dead." Source of quote: *Annie Allen:* Greenwood Press, Westport, CT. 1971. Reprint edition. The golden shovel is a poetic form created by Terrence Hayes in 2010 in honor of Brooks.

"Metamorphosis" centers on lymphedema, a common condition caused by breast cancer surgery. Treatment involves seeing an occupational therapist (OT) and bandaging the arm to reduce swelling of lymph nodes. Sometimes the condition is permanent.

"The Second Arrow"—epigraph from the poem "Faith" by Czeslaw Milosz. *All Poetry.* Web. The last stanza of the piece references Buddhist mystic Thich Nhat Hanh and his article, "The Second Arrow."

"Amazons." Some details from this poem come from *National Geographic.*

"The Healer." Some details in this poem were inspired by an exhibit of Brazilian artist Tarsila do Amaral at the Art Institute of Chicago, in particular the 1923 painting "A Negra."

"Blood Falls"—This poem was inspired by Delaney Ross's online article, "What's Really in Antarctica's Mysterious Blood Falls." *National Geographic,* 22 Oct. 2018. Online.

"My Wound"—I taught English in Budapest, Hungary, for one year, 1991–92. Some images from my experience appear in this poem.

"Modlitwa"—Epigraph taken from the poem, "A Few Words on the Soul," by Polish poet Wislawa Szymborska. "Modlitwa" is a haibun, which is a hybrid mix of prose poetry and haiku originally created in Japan in the 17th century. "The Other Garden" and "Freedom" are also haibun.

"Prayer" includes references to French poet Paul Verlaine's poem, "Clair de Lune," and Claude Debussy's classical song of the same name.

"The Language of Cancer" won 2nd Place in a national 2023 contest on the theme of healing, transformation, and cancer. It was published in 2024 on the LIGHT journal website, Light4ph.org (Leaders Igniting Generational Healing and Transformation).

"Refuge"—The Willowbrook Wildlife Center, now called the DuPage Wildlife Conservation Center, is a haven in suburban Chicago for injured and orphaned wild animals.

"Rowing" was inspired by Chilean poet Pablo Neruda's poem, "Walking Around."

"Sonography of a Survivor"—Adriamycin and Taxol are types of chemotherapy.

"To the 800,000 DACA Children, from One Cancer Survivor"—DACA stands for Deferred Action for Childhood Arrivals and is an immigration policy created by then U.S. president Barack Obama on June 12, 2012, allowing some young undocumented people legal status to live and work in the U.S.

"At the Plaza del Carmen in Madrid" includes references to Spanish poet Frederico Garcia Lorca, who was killed in 1936 during the reign of Francisco "Franco" Bahamonde's dictatorship.

About the Author

Nominated for a Pushcart Prize and Best of the Net, Caroline Johnson has two illustrated poetry chapbooks, *Where the Street Ends* and *My Mother's Artwork,* and a full-length collection, *The Caregiver* (Holy Cow! Press, 2018). She has won numerous local and national awards for her poetry, including the 2012 *Chicago Tribune*'s Printers Row Poetry Contest. Her work can be found in Garrison Keillor's *Writer's Almanac, Origins Journal, Ekphrastic Review, Naugatuck River Review, Encore, Pink Panther Magazine,* and *After Hours,* among others.

A former college English teacher, she has led workshops for veterans and other poets on topics such as Poetry and Spirituality, Speculative Poetry, and Writing About Chicago. She is past president and current treasurer of Poets & Patrons of Chicago and a member of the P2 Collective, a Chicago-area group of poets and photographers who present at galleries and online.

Visit her at:
caroline-johnson.com

www.ingramcontent.com/pod-product-compliance
Lightning Source LLC
Chambersburg PA
CBHW072156160426
43197CB00012B/2411